"The day I found my forever home." – Minna
Take My Paw Rescue in Fowlerville, Michigan - March 15, 2014
Thank you to all the organizations who care enough to give animals a second chance at life.

by Erica Abel

illustrated by Rachel McCoy

This book is dedicated to...

To my mom and dad for always believing in me and teaching me the joy of writing.

To the other three Whimsical Writers for going on this adventurous endeavor with me!

And, of course, to my sweet, spit fire of a rescue dog, Minna. Without her spirit and story, this book would not exist.

-Erica

To my favorite spring-loaded dachshund, Sasha. Your life was too short, but lived to its very fullest. No trashcan went unturned while you were here, no hose un-barked at, and not a single snake was ever left in sight.

-Rachel

Text copyright © 2018 by Erica Abel
Illustrations copyright © 2018 by Rachel McCoy
Edited by Nora Cohen
All rights reserved.

Published in the United States of America by Whimsical Writers, Grand Rapids, Michigan.
Printed by Grandville Printing Company, Grandville, Michigan.

No part of this book may be used or reproduced in any form without written permission from the publisher, Whimsical Writers, 615 Jackson St., Grandville, MI 49418.

Minna and the Canine Club is a registered trademark of The Whimsical Writers.
Visit us on the Web!
www.minnaandthecanineclub.com

Library of Congress Cataloging-in-Publication Data
Library of Congress Control Number: 2018907818

ISBN: 978-0-9993378-0-6

It all started one September morning on my favorite green chair, in my friendly neighborhood. Well, except for the guy next door who loves to grill hot dogs and doesn't give me one nibble.

I'm Minna, and that's with a long "I" — like in the word "line" when a teacher says, "Line up, everyone!"

Whenever people meet me, they think I am pretty adorable, which is correct. What they *don't* know is that I am *more* than just a dog.

I am a fashionista …

a detective …

Oh, and we cannot forget that I am also a humanitarian. That means I care about others.

"What? I was just helping him collect more acorns!"

There was one thing I was *not*, however. I was not a teacher. Not *yet*, that is.

Every morning, I see my human pack her gray canvas bag with books and pencils. I always try to dig into that bag — you know, just to make sure that everything is properly packed up. Of course, I always make sure I'm not missing a delicious treat hidden in there.

Then, after my human puts on her shoes and coat, she heads out the door to school. You see, she is a teacher.

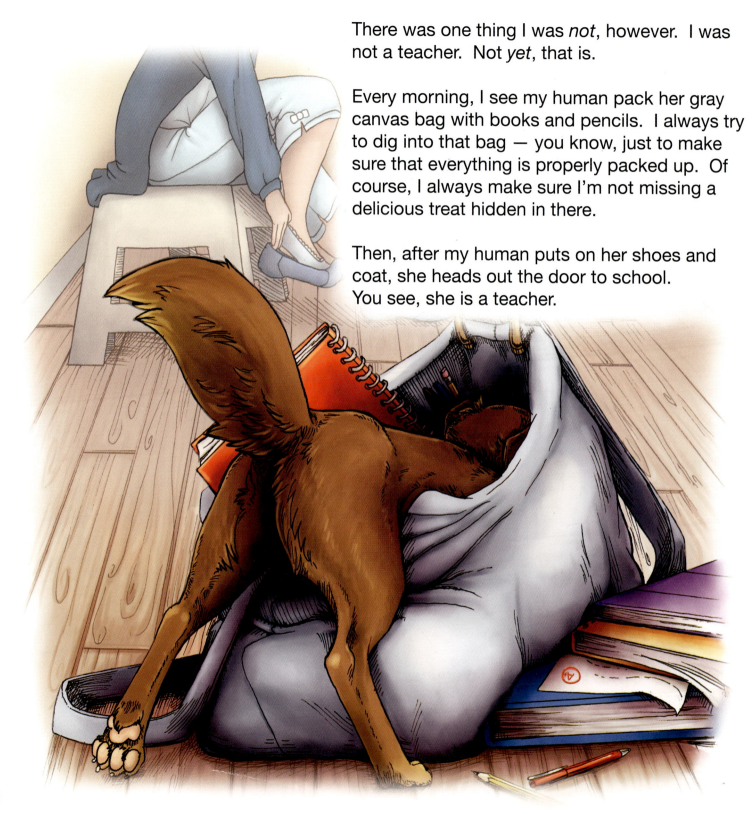

One day as my human left for work carrying her book bag out the door, I thought to myself, School must be interesting. Suddenly, an idea came to me. I thought that it was about time someone started educating the canines in this neighborhood. That was when I decided I would start my own school.

I knew that the first thing I had to do was to get some students. I jumped down from my green chair, where I spent hours napping and dreaming, and headed outside.

I went to the backyard fence, and barked out an invitation to my gal pal Maggie to join my school. Maggie did a happy dance.

Maggie has been my friend since my human and I moved in next door. Maggie is *almost* as mischievous as me. The two of us have met under the fence every night, nose to nose, to discuss important events — like what shoes and toilet paper we have chewed that day.

"Maybe you can bring some treats to my new school," I suggested hopefully, licking my lips in anticipation.

"I think that can be arranged," Maggie replied, with a twinkle in her eye.

Next, I invited my uncle, Blue, a husky who lived down the block. Blue is wise and dependable. He always stands up to the bully-dogs in the neighborhood. Blue said he would definitely come to school.

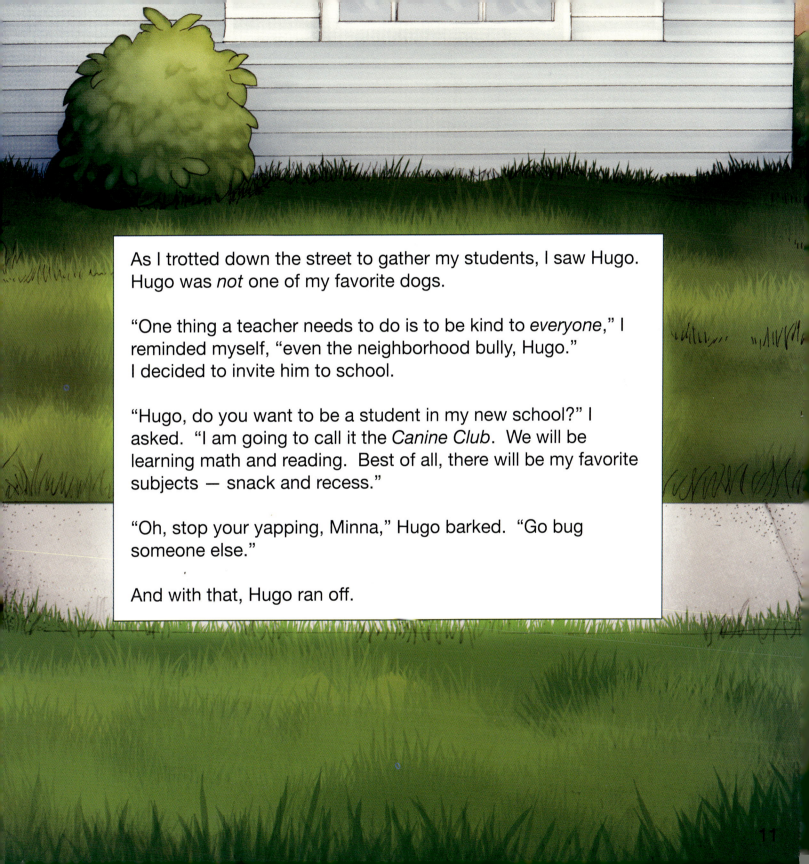

As I trotted down the street to gather my students, I saw Hugo. Hugo was *not* one of my favorite dogs.

"One thing a teacher needs to do is to be kind to *everyone*," I reminded myself, "even the neighborhood bully, Hugo." I decided to invite him to school.

"Hugo, do you want to be a student in my new school?" I asked. "I am going to call it the *Canine Club*. We will be learning math and reading. Best of all, there will be my favorite subjects — snack and recess."

"Oh, stop your yapping, Minna," Hugo barked. "Go bug someone else."

And with that, Hugo ran off.

He was no flea off my back. Right then and there I created my first rule on how to lead a classy and fabulous life.

Rule 1 to Lead a Classy and Fabulous Life:

Follow your dreams no matter what! Don't let others dull your diamonds.

As Blue and I walked down the street, we saw Blue's friend Clancy racing up to us from his yard.

"Hey, Clancy — do you want to join Minna's new school?" Blue asked him.

"Oh, no!" Clancy answered nervously. "I don't think I can do school."

"Sure, you can! School will be fun, Clancy," Blue reassured him.

"Well, do you think I will make any friends?" Clancy whispered shyly.

"Clancy, of course you will!" I replied gently. "You are kind and full of imagination, and you already have us as your friends!"

"I don't know," Clancy said. "But I'll come today and try it out."

I led my new students to the front of my human's garage. It had a broken door that didn't completely shut at the bottom.

"This is the perfect place to have a classroom for our Canine Club!" I announced. I wiggled my body under the garage door and, *voila*, I was in my new classroom. I peered under and called, "Come on in!"

Clancy looked nervous. Blue gave him the last nudge he needed, and the dogs squeezed under the door.

"Canine Club, listen up!" I said in my best teacher voice. "It has come to my attention that we canines are missing out on one of life's greatest journeys—learning. My human has been teaching miniature humans about numbers and letters. I think it is about time that we canines learn those things, too!"

"But what are numbers?" Clancy asked, confused.

"Well, Clancy, I will be glad to teach you all about numbers! I've been learning about them by listening to my human."

Suddenly, there was a long bark coming from next door. *"ARRROOOOO!"*

"Dazzling diamonds!" I said in alarm. "That sounds like my gal pal Maggie. She must be on the other side of the fence next door!"

With that, we all wiggled back under the garage door.

We could hear Maggie whimpering from the other side.

"Minna? Blue? Clancy?" Maggie called out.

"Maggie, are you stuck there behind your fence?" I asked.

"Yes, Minna, I am in my yard and I can't get over to your side! What am I going to do?" Maggie asked.

A rude voice chimed in, "Ha! You mutts *still* trying to start a school?" Hugo asked, laughing. "That will *never* happen. Look, Minna, you already left one of your students behind!"

"Hugo, I thought you left?"

Hugo only laughed and left his mark on the fire hydrant in front of the house.

"Don't listen to him, Minna," Blue said. "We can do anything we put our paws to."

"Canines, tails up!" I said, turning away from Hugo. "We have a problem and we must focus. We need to get Maggie over here. Before we can start school, we need to have all canines with us in the classroom."

The first day of school was *not* going as planned. Blue, Clancy, and I sat there thinking about how we could get Maggie over here.

"Minna, maybe we could run and hit the fence really hard to knock it down," Clancy suggested shyly. "Then Maggie could come join us."

"Clancy, that is a great idea!" Blue said.

"I am willing to try anything," I said. "Let's line ourselves up, and on the count of three we will run and hit the fence together. Maggie, watch out!" I called.

"One … two … three!" everyone barked as we ran toward the fence.

Three dogs on the ground. But the fence was still standing.

"Hahahaha!" Hugo laughed.

"Well, thanks for trying," Maggie called out from behind the fence. "Maybe I just can't come to school today."

"No! We are the Canine Club and we do not give up!" I said firmly. "And we do not leave anyone out. That includes you, Hugo — you are still welcome to join us."

"Exactly," Blue agreed.

But Hugo just looked surprised and didn't answer.

"What are we going to do now? I guess my idea wasn't very good," Clancy said sadly.

"Clancy, don't say that! You were brave to come up with that idea," I said.

"Tails back up, canines! Back to brainstorming," Blue said.

Tick tock, tick tock, tick tock. The garden clock in Maggie's yard reminded me that time was ticking away. I started to lose hope that I would ever get my friend to school.

"Hey, maybe we can build a dog ladder and jump over the fence," I suggested.

So, with strong and sturdy Blue on the bottom, Clancy in the middle, and me on top, we created a ladder. But when I got to the top, ready to jump to Maggie, I could feel Clancy shaking.

"Clancy? Are you okay?" I asked.

"I … I … think I'm going to …" choked Clancy.

And without another word, the dog ladder collapsed.

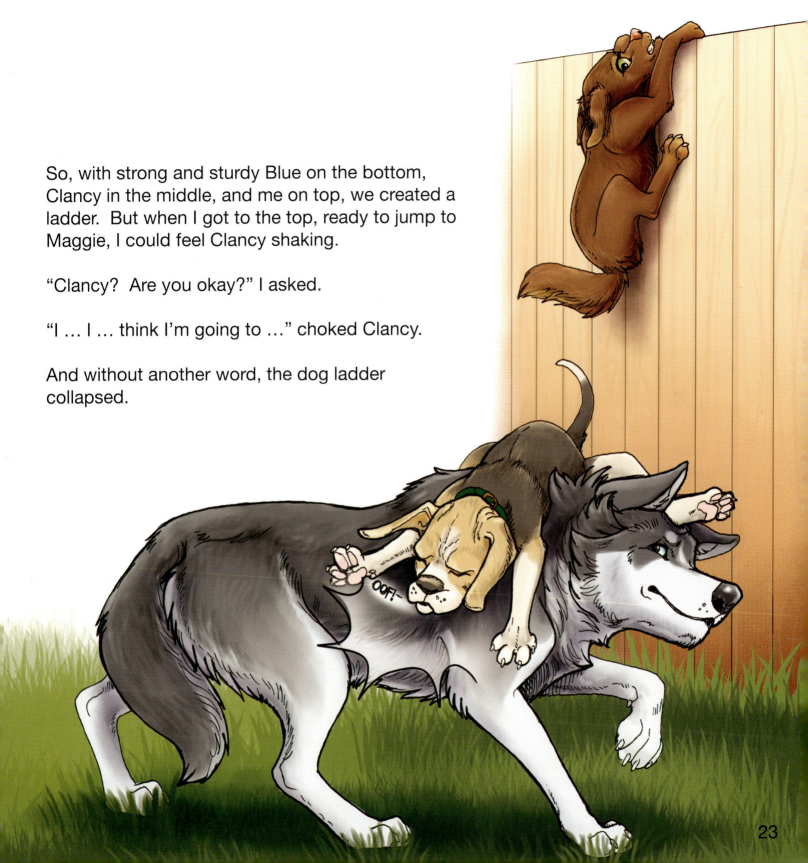

"Are you guys alright?" Maggie asked.

"Yes, we are okay," I said. "I am so sorry I let you down, Maggie. You and I can just meet under the fence tonight and talk like we usually do. We will have to dig a deeper hole, though. I can barely see your whiskers!"

"I guess the Canine Club will have to go on without me today," Maggie sighed.

"Wait," Blue said. His face suddenly lit up as if his human was about to give him a whole pizza. "What did you say about digging a hole under the fence to meet up?" he asked.

"Maggie and I always have to dig a deeper hole so we can chat through a space under the fence," I said slowly. "Our humans keep filling it in whenever they notice it."

"Minna, don't you see?" Blue said. "If we can just dig a deep enough hole, Maggie can crawl under it and get to school! The Canine Club will go on!"

"Blue, you are so smart!" Clancy barked.

"Canines, it's time to dig!" I shouted.

The three of us took turns digging rapidly. Dirt was flying faster than you could say *dazzling diamonds*.

"You are doing it! The hole is getting bigger!" Maggie called out from the other side, dancing around in circles.

Blue's big paws scooped out the last of the dirt and before anyone knew it, Maggie squeezed her body right under the fence to join us.

"I'm here!" she announced.

The Canine Club howled and cheered. "We did it!"

"Thank you for getting me to school! You dogs are the best pup pals a girl could ask for," Maggie said.

"Well, we could not have done it without everyone's help," Blue said. "When we put our paws together anything is possible."

"You are right, Blue," I said. "I am so glad all of my students are here. Now, let's put a big flowerpot over the hole so our humans don't find it. I think it's officially time for school to be in session. But first, some pizza for our hard work! I've got that covered."

And with that, we ran into our new classroom.

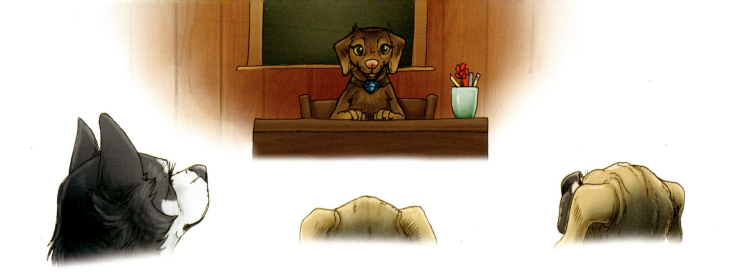

"Canines, I think we'd better get started with some learning," I began.

Suddenly, the town church bells rang.

GONG. GONG. GONG. GONG.

Everyone looked at each other. Four o'clock meant that our humans would be coming home soon.

"It looks like we won't have time for any learning today," Clancy declared.

"Actually, Clancy," Blue barked, "I think we did learn something today — work together as a team and never give up!"

"And reward yourself with pizza for a job well done!" Maggie said, giggling.

"Tomorrow, we can start with math, but for now, every pup back to your dog beds!" I shouted, giving my final teacher order of the day.

Every tail in the garage started wagging and every Canine Club member raced home as we sang,

*"We are the Canine Club!
To help is our duty.
We patrol the neighborhood
To keep peace and beauty."*

I made it back home without a second to spare. I tip-pawed back to my green chair and curled up against the soft cushions. I closed my eyes tightly. When my human walked through the door a moment later, I opened my eyes and barked hello to greet her.

"Minna, have you been sleeping all day?" she asked, chuckling. She fussed over me, petting me and rubbing behind my ears as she put down her book bag.

"I bet you had a quiet day, huh?" she asked. "We'd better take you out for a walk and get you some fresh air, and then I want some of that leftover pizza!"

Oh no! I giggled to myself. It wasn't exactly a quiet day, and I had a feeling it wouldn't be a quiet night, either.

Teaching Points

Reading is one of the most important skills a child will learn. Children begin by learning to read and then they read to learn. The love of reading is just as important as the process of reading. It is our hope that children will enjoy reading *Minna and the Canine Club*, and will love and appreciate the adorable canines in the story. We have included skills that can be taught as you share this book with your child or your class. These skills will not only enhance understanding of this book, but also help children become better readers. Make your children's reading a more rewarding experience by using this page as a reference to teach necessary reading skills and strategies.

Comprehension:

- Retell (**summarize**) the story in his or her own words
- Identify the **main characters, setting, problem, solution**
- Identify who is telling the story (**Point of View:** first, second, or third person)
- **Compare & Contrast:** Identify similarities and differences for the following: characters and actions or reactions of the characters. Children could create a Venn diagram.
- Identify the **Author's Purpose** (entertain, inform, or persuade)
- Explain **Cause and Effect** relationships
- Identify the **Theme**

Vocabulary:

adorable .... p. 3	canines .... p. 7	dependable ..... p. 10	dazzling .... p. 16
nibble .... p. 3	mischievous ..... p. 9	definitely ..... p. 10	whimpering .... p. 16
fashionista ..... p. 4	suggested .... p. 9	classy .... p. 12	rude .... p. 17
detective .... p. 4	anticipation ..... p. 9	fabulous .... p. 12	sturdy .... p. 23
humanitarian ... p. 5	arranged .... p. 9	peered .... p. 14	collapsed ..... p. 23
canvas .... p. 6	invited .... p. 10	nudge .... p. 14	barely .... p. 24
properly .... p. 6	wise .... p. 10	miniature ...... p. 15	

- Use **context clues** in the text for the meaning of the vocabulary word
- Identify the **part of speech** for vocabulary words (noun, verb, adjective, adverb)
- Identify words or phrases that show **feelings** or appeal to the **senses**
- Name a **synonym or antonym** for the vocabulary word
- Practice **dictionary skills** by looking up the words and using them in a sentence

Literary Devices:

- onomatopoeia: p. 17 *ARRROOOOO*; p. 22 *THUD, THUD, THUD*; p. 24 *tick tock, tick tock*; p. 30 *GONG. GONG. GONG.*
- antagonist: introduced on page 8 (Hugo)
- idiom: p 13 *Go bug someone else*; p. 13 *no flea off my back, dull your diamonds*
- alliteration: p. 18 and 27 *dazzling diamonds*

More detailed lessons and activities are available on the website at: www.minnaandthecanineclub.com.